AF225795

ANGRY ARTHUR

and the Run Around Trick

Kindful Kids Books

This Kindful Kids book belongs to:

First Published in 2025 by Kindful Kids Books

ISBN: 978-1-0683378-1-9 (hardback)
ISBN: 978-1-0683378-0-2 (paperback)

Stories to help children understand their big feelings,
created from the heart to support young minds.

Disclaimer: This book is intended for educational
purposes. It is not a substitute for professional
advice, diagnosis, or treatment. If you have
concerns about your child's emotional well-being,
please consult a qualified professional.

Arthur sat at his desk, staring at the maths questions in front of him. None of them made sense. He kept getting the answers wrong—*nothing was going right today!*

It had already been a tough morning.
He'd woken up late—again. His sister
had eaten all his favourite cereal,
leaving him with porridge—*yuk!*

His dinosaur lunchbox was nowhere
to be found, and just as his dad was
rushing him to get in the car,
he realised he'd forgotten
his library book.

And now this? His cheeks felt hot as he stared down at the numbers. "This is so stupid," he muttered, pressing down until—crack—his pencil tip snapped. *Why is maths always so confusing?*

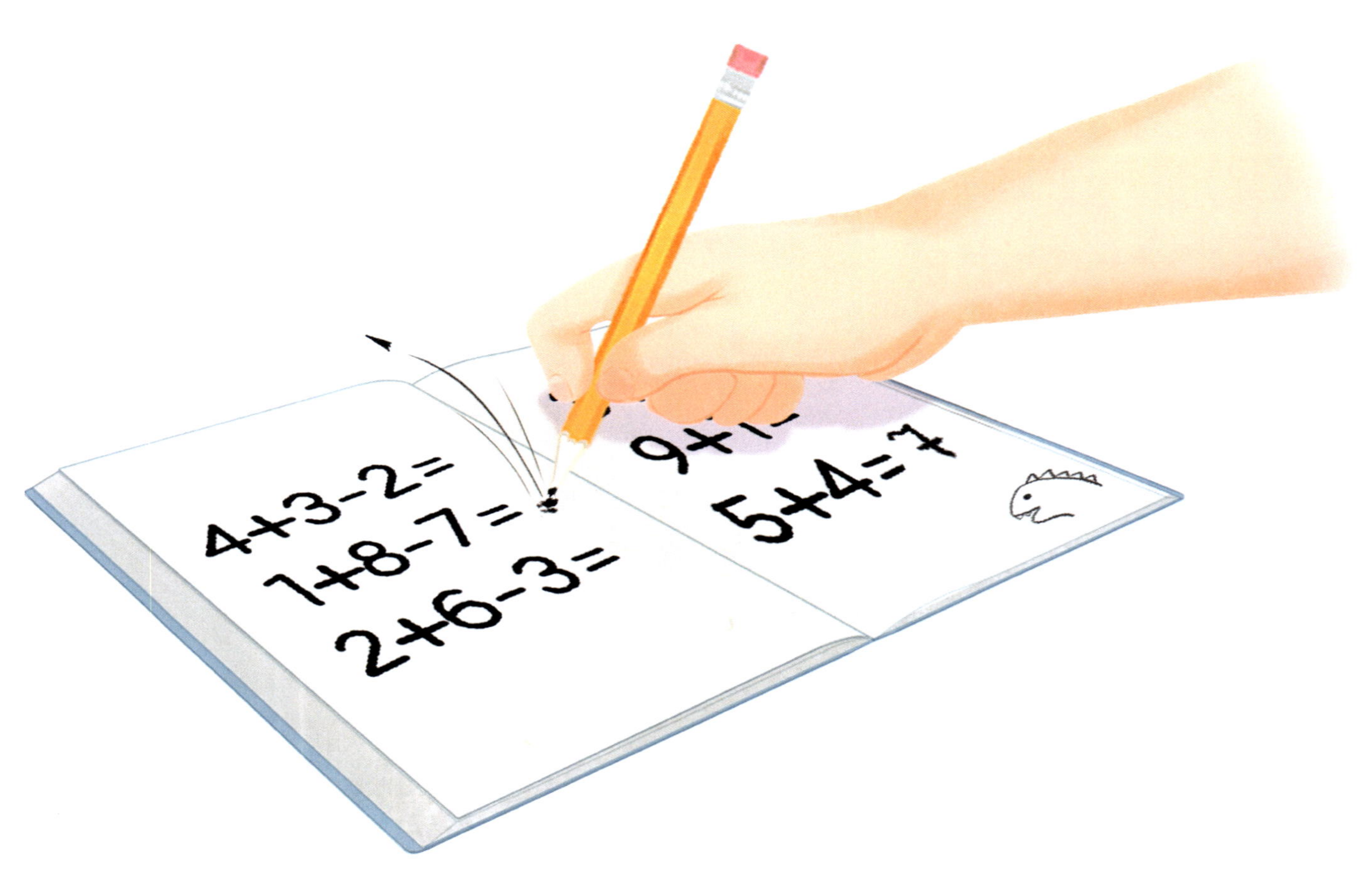
4+3-2=
1+8-7=
2+6-3=
9+
5+4=7

He sat frozen, red-faced, fists clenched. Have you ever felt so frustrated that even little things, like a broken pencil, make you feel like you might explode? That's exactly how Arthur felt right now.

Miss Wisewood noticed Arthur's red cheeks.
She could tell it was one of those days when
he was struggling and needed a distraction.

Arthur sat gripping the edge of the desk tightly,
his feet banging against the chair legs.
Miss Wisewood knew just what to do.

"All right, class!" Miss Wisewood said with a smile, clapping her hands. "We're taking a quick break—everyone outside!"

The class looked at each other in surprise, then sprang
to their feet. Arthur groaned, dragging himself to the door.
What good will this do?

Outside, Miss Wisewood gathered the class in a circle.
"All right, everyone! We're going to run on the spot as fast as we can," she said. "Run until it feels like all that extra energy disappears!"

Arthur stood with his arms crossed, frowning as his friends
started running, their feet thumping up and down on
the ground. Peter and Eva were giggling as they sped up.
Arthur watched, feeling his frustration growing inside him.
He didn't think anything would make him feel better.

But his legs felt restless,
like they wanted to move.

Slowly, Arthur took one step, then another, and before he knew it, he was running too! His legs moved faster, energy flowed through him. With each step, the tight feeling in his body began to loosen.

Bit by bit, his anger and frustration faded away, his racing thoughts slowing until, for the first time that day, his mind was still.
Did you know that moving your body can sometimes help you feel better when you're angry? Arthur hadn't realised that before, but now, his whole body felt lighter.

After a few minutes, most of the children began to slow down, catching their breath. But Arthur's legs kept moving until Miss Wisewood finally called everyone to stop.

"Now let's slow it right down," Miss Wisewood said softly.
She took a long breath in, lifting her shoulders slowly,
and then out, relaxing them. Arthur joined in, taking a deep
breath, and started to calm down.

He looked around and saw a peaceful stillness
had settled over everyone, himself included!

Back in the classroom, Miss Wisewood had everyone lie on the floor. "Now, we're going to help our bodies and minds relax completely," she instructed gently. Arthur lay down and noticed the warmth in his face had cooled.

"Let's start by clenching our toes," she said in a quiet voice.
Arthur squeezed his toes tightly. "And let go," Miss Wisewood
said, and he relaxed them. They moved through each part
of their bodies, clenching and relaxing, from their toes
to their heads—even their cheeks and eyes!

With each deep breath, Arthur felt his whole body soften,
and the last bit of tension melted away. He couldn't help
but smile a little. He hadn't known he could feel this good.

When they returned to their desks, Arthur felt better than he had all day. Feeling focused and ready, he started working on his maths again.

William glanced over and gave him a thumbs-up.
"Nice work, Arthur!" Arthur smiled back, proud of himself
for trying his best.

As Arthur packed his bag, he thought about his frustration earlier and wondered, *Why do I get so angry when things don't go my way?* But he remembered how much better he felt after running and realised he could calm himself, even on tough days.

Maybe next time I start to feel angry, I can try moving first,
he thought, feeling hopeful. Arthur had learnt that sometimes,
a little movement—or relaxing his body—was all he needed
to feel better.

And guess what? The very next time Arthur felt those big emotions bubbling up, he remembered Miss Wisewood's running trick. Before the strong feelings could take over, he let his legs move—and the frustration started to slip away.

It felt so good to know that sometimes, the best way to calm his mind was to move his body. *I don't have to stay angry, he thought with a smile. I just need to move!*

Teacher & Parent Guide

This story helps children build emotional intelligence by recognising big feelings and practising simple techniques to manage them. In this story, Arthur learns how moving his body can help him manage anger and feel calm.

Here's how to practise this technique with children:

Physical Release: Encourage children to run on the spot as fast as they can for 30 seconds to one minute. Invite them to imagine any heavy feelings floating away as they move. This active movement helps release built-up energy and tension.

Progressive Muscle Relaxation: Once children have slowed down, guide them to lie on the floor or sit comfortably. Lead them through the relaxation exercise.

♥ *Instructions*: Clench and squeeze your toes tightly, then let go. Move slowly through each part of your body, first tense and then relax it completely. Don't forget to breathe!

♥ Ask children to notice how they feel.

Variation – Slowing Down: For quieter moments, guide the children to slow down their movements after running and take a few deep breaths. Encourage them to notice their heartbeat and how they feel in their body.

Discussion Points for Building Emotional Awareness

These gentle questions can help children reflect on their experiences and build emotional awareness:

♥ Have you ever felt as angry as Arthur? What did you do to feel better?

♥ How did moving his body make Arthur feel different? Do you think running or relaxing could help you when you're frustrated?

♥ Can you think of other ways to help your body feel calm, like Arthur's running or relaxing trick?

♥ How could you help a friend who is feeling angry or frustrated?

Here we are!

Did you find us all?

William   Eva   Brian

Mouse

Biscuit

Remember every feeling is telling a story -

keep listening to yours ♥